# TREE OF LIFE

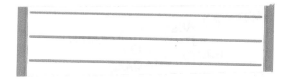

# TREE OF LIFE
## The World of the African Baobab

## BARBARA BASH

Sierra Club Books | Little, Brown and Company
San Francisco | Boston • Toronto • London

To my parents,
and to all the people who are
fighting to save the vitality
of the African ecosystem

The author wishes to thank the National Museum of Kenya for its
help in researching information for this book.

The Sierra Club, founded in 1892 by John Muir, has devoted itself to the study
and protection of the earth's scenic and ecological resources — mountains, wet-
lands, woodlands, wild shores and rivers, deserts and plains. The publishing
program of the Sierra Club offers books to the public as a nonprofit educational
service in the hope that they may enlarge the public's understanding of the Club's
basic concerns. The Sierra Club has some sixty chapters in the United States and
in Canada. For information about how you may participate in its programs to
preserve wilderness and the quality of life, please address inquiries to Sierra Club,
730 Polk Street, San Francisco, CA 94109.

First Edition

All calligraphy by Barbara Bash

Library of Congress Cataloging-in-Publication Data

Bash, Barbara.
        Tree of life: the world of the African baobab / Barbara Bash. — 1st ed.
            p.    cm. — (Tree tales)
        Summary: Text and pictures document the life cycle of this
        amazing tree of the African savannah, and portrays the animals
        and people it helps to support.
        ISBN 0-316-08305-4 (Little, Brown)
    1. Baobab — Africa — Ecology — Juvenile literature.
    2. Baobab — Africa — Life cycle — Juvenile literature.
    3. Savanna ecology — Africa — Juvenile literature.
    [1. Baobab.   2. Trees.   3. Africa.   4. Ecology.]   I. Title.
    II. Series.
    QK495.B7B37 1989
    583′.19 — dc19                              89-6028
                                                  CIP
                                                  AC


10   9   8   7   6   5   4   3   2   1

Sierra Club Books/Little, Brown children's books are published by Little,
Brown and Company (Inc.) in association with Sierra Club Books.

Published simultaneously in Canada by
Little, Brown & Company (Canada) Limited

Printed in the United States of America

In the oldest times, as the !Kung
Bushmen of Africa tell the story,
the Great Spirit gave each animal
a tree to plant. Hyena arrived late
and was given the very last tree,
the baobab. Being a careless
creature, he planted it upside
down—and that is why its
branches look like gnarled roots.

The baobab grows on the dry savannahs of Africa. Reaching crookedly into the air, it stands silent and ancient. Many people believe there are no young baobabs – that they spring into being full grown. Perhaps this is because the young, slender trees look so different from the older ones. They begin to thicken and twist after forty years of growth and can eventually measure up to forty feet across and sixty feet high. With a life span of more than one thousand years, baobabs outlive nearly everything on earth.

Sour Gourd Tree, Cream of Tartar Tree, Monkey Bread Tree, the Elephant of Plants – there are many names for the baobab. The African people also give each old baobab its own special name beginning with "Um," which means Mother. For them, the baobab is filled with mystery, and they honor it like an elder.

For most of the year the baobab stands leafless and bare, but twice a year the rains come, and for a brief period the tree leafs out and blooms. Sometimes even before the rains begin, the baobab senses the coming moisture and sends out its soft new leaves and flower buds.

Soon birds arrive to make their nests in the baobab's hollows. The yellow-collared lovebird and the mosque swallow perch in the high branches. The old tree starts to hum with life.

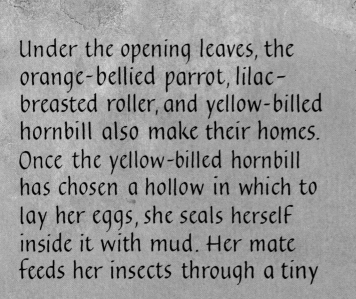

Under the opening leaves, the orange-bellied parrot, lilac-breasted roller, and yellow-billed hornbill also make their homes. Once the yellow-billed hornbill has chosen a hollow in which to lay her eggs, she seals herself inside it with mud. Her mate feeds her insects through a tiny slit for more than six weeks. Then, when the eggs have hatched and the babies are large, she breaks out of her crowded, protective prison. The chicks rebuild the damaged hole and are fed by their parents for three more weeks, until it's time for them to break out and fly.

Sweat bees

Longhorn
beetle

Soon after the rains begin, the
baobab is full of activity. Tiny
sweat bees build slender tunnels
leading to their hives inside the
tree. The cotton bollworm eats the
baobab wood, while the longhorn
beetle, elegant grasshopper, and
Masonga caterpillar munch the
foliage. In the center of the tender
leaves, cotton stainer bugs, flea
beetles, and long-tailed mealybugs
cluster and chew.

Elegant grasshopper

Cotton
bollworm

Long-tailed
mealybug

Flea
beetle

Cotton
stainer
bug

Masonga
caterpillar

At twilight, the large white flowers begin to open. Small furry creatures called bushbabies emerge from their hollows in the tree and smell the sweet nectar. They dart from branch to branch like little elves, pushing their faces into the flowers, lapping up the nectar, and carrying the sticky yellow pollen on to the next bloom. The soft leaves rustle as the bushbabies chirp and scurry about.

Deep in the night, the fruit bats
arrive to drink the flower nectar,
too. The mothers fly with their
young pups holding on to their fur.
The restless fluttering goes on all
night. Standing under the dark
tree, one might think there were
spirits in the baobab branches.

In the morning, the flowers that opened the night before have fallen to the ground, and a pair of eland comes to lap up the soft petals. A trio of impalas also munches the petals quietly, keeping a watchful eye on the horizon for signs of danger. No one seems to notice the tiny dik-dik that hides in the lush grass nearby. In the distance, a lone giraffe reaches for the baobab's tender leaves.

In a few weeks, the rains end and the baobab's leaves begin to fall, exposing the weaver nests. The male red-headed weaver has been weaving a hanging nest with a long entrance spout at the end of a branch, while the buffalo weaver has built a spiky clump of twigs. Both nests protect the birds' eggs from dangerous snakes. When the nests are complete, the male weavers attract females to the new homes they've built. But if the females don't like the nests, the males must start all over again! The tree is full of weaver nests, and the birds dart busily in and out.

When all the leaves have fallen,
the fruit begins to develop. Soon
hundreds of big melon shapes
hang from the bare branches.
Before long, a family of baboons
arrives to feast on the fresh fruit.

They spend the whole day in the
baobab, cracking open the hard
velvety shells and scooping out the
sweet pulp of all the fruit they can
reach. Seeds fall to the ground as
the baboons scamper and chortle.

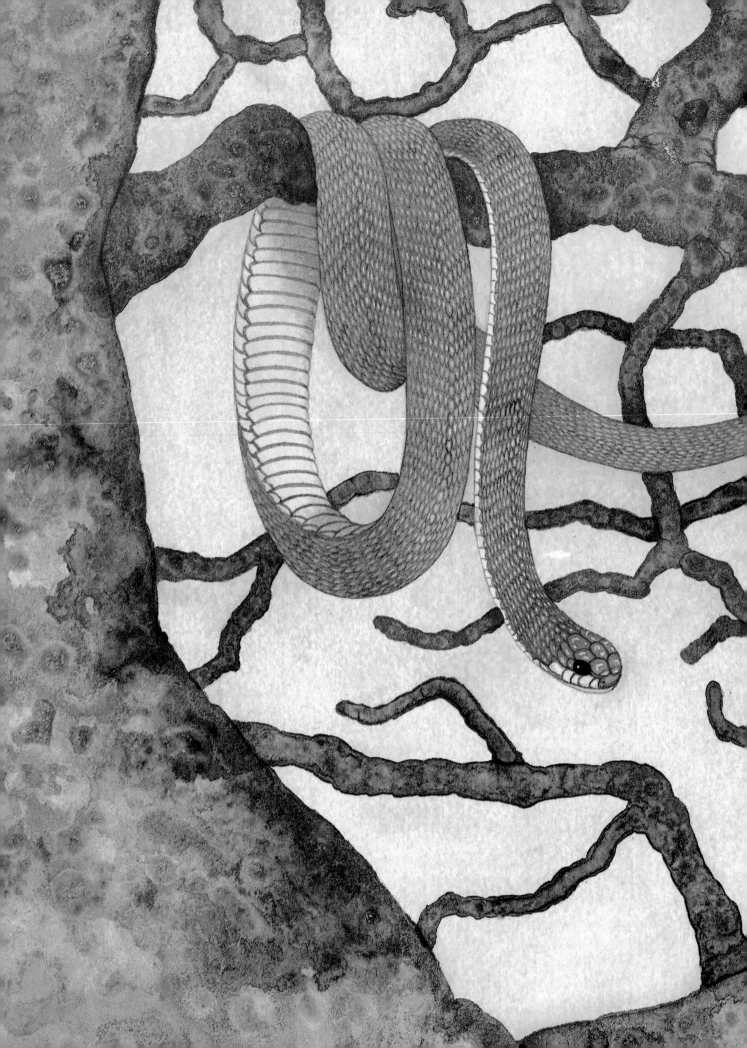

After the fruit is gone, the baobab is very still. A boomslang snake drapes its long body over a gnarled branch and waits. A praying mantis turns its head, its large eyes ever-watchful. A stick insect hides from the snake in plain sight, looking very much like a twig. A flap-eared chameleon is also camouflaged in the branches; it turns the color of its surroundings and does not move.

Sometimes the stillness is broken by the call of the honey guide bird—*aje-je-je-je*—and the voices of tribesmen who follow close behind. The bird dips and swoops, flashing its white tail feathers, until it gets close to a hive in the baobab. Then the honey guide perches quietly nearby and waits for the hunters to find the hive. The men climb the baobab, smoke out the bees, and scoop out the honey. But they always leave some beeswax behind, as thanks to the honey guide bird.

To the African people, the baobab is more than a source of honey. Its bark is stripped for baskets and rope; its fruit is made into candy and sweet drinks; and its roots and leaves are used as medicine. On the hot, dry savannah, the hollow trunks of ancient baobabs can also become water containers and even shelters.

At the end of the long, dry season, the thirsty elephants arrive and begin to eat the baobab bark, extracting juices from the soft fiber. With their enormous strength, the elephants strip away all the bark and pull down large chunks of wood, leaving gaping holes in the trunk. But the baobab heals its wounds, produces new bark, and keeps growing.

Finally, after many, many years, the old baobab dies. Perhaps too many elephants have chewed the wood and weakened its structure, or insects have broken down its inner core.

One day it collapses in on itself, a melted heap of ruins. Over time, only a soft mound of powdery fragments is left. The wind will blow these away until nothing of the baobab remains.

In the sky, the clouds begin to build
for the coming rains. Near the dust
of the dead tree, a baobab seed has
sprouted. It is all alone on the wide
savannah. Now the story of the
baobab begins all over again.